Exploring Venus and Mercury

Today's World in Space

Exploring Venus and Mercury

By David Baker

Rourke Enterprises, Inc.
Vero Beach, FL 32964

Library of Congress Cataloging-in-Publication Data
Baker, David, 1944-
    Exploring Venus and Mercury/by David Baker.
    p. cm — (Today's world in space)
    Includes index.
    Summary: Chronicles NASA's exploration of Venus and Mercury, describing the missions and scientific discoveries made by Mariner and Pioneer.
    ISBN 0-86592-371-X
    1. Venus (Planet) — Juvenile literature. 2. Mercury (Planet) — Juvenile literature. 3. Planets — Exploration — Juvenile literature.
[1. Venus (Planet) 2. Mercury (Planet) 3. Planets — Exploration.]
I. Title. II. Series: Baker, David, 1944- Today's world space.
QB621.B25   1989   88-33707
523.4'1 - dc19   CIP
                                                          AC

523.4/B   c. 1   6/91 $12.95

CONTENTS

The Solar System

From the earliest days when humans first looked toward the stars, they were aware of certain lights in the sky that seemed at times brighter than the rest. These lights moved quickly across the heavens and appeared to have a wandering life of their own. Over time, scientists came to realize that the brighter, moving lights were those that were closer to Earth, while the remaining lights were farther away.

With the invention of the telescope in the early seventeenth century and the dawn of a new age of science, it was possible to unravel the mystery. The nearer lights were planets, and like Earth, they moved around the sun. The more distant lights were stars, which were so far away that they appeared almost without motion. As people learned more, the size of the universe fell into place.

The Earth, scientists discovered, is about 93 million miles from the sun. Earth's companion moon is less than 240,000 miles away. It takes light eight minutes to get from the sun to the Earth, but only slightly more than one second to get from Earth to the moon. Such is the enormous distance between the sun and the Earth. By the 1930s, eight other planets had been discovered. Most of these were known to ancient astronomers, who had only their naked eyes for viewing the sky. When telescopes were invented, the rest of the planets were discovered.

From a Viking spacecraft the surface of Mars is visible to the human eye but Venus is totally shrouded in dense cloud; Mercury is too close to the sun to see surface features from Earth.

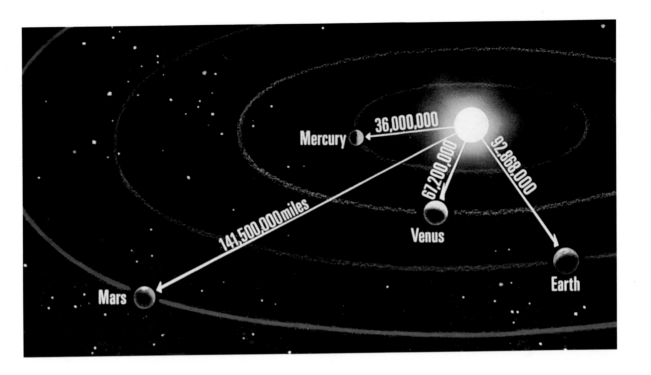

The four terrestrial planets of the solar system are Mercury, Venus, Earth, and Mars.

The outer planets of the solar system begin with giant Jupiter, seen here in this imaginary landscape from its moon, Ganymede.

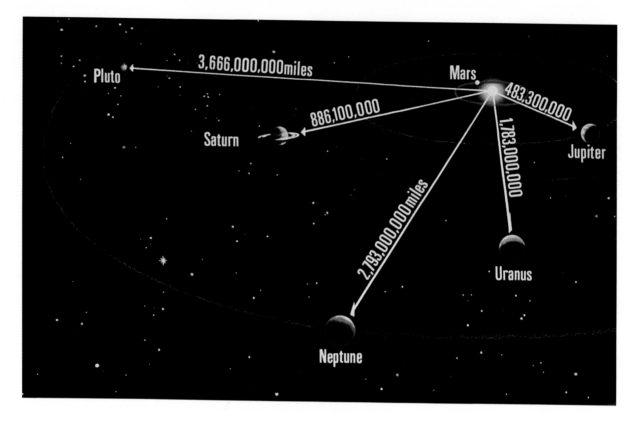

The outer planets stretch far into the distant regions of the solar system and include Jupiter, Saturn, Uranus, Neptune, and tiny Pluto.

Smaller than Saturn, Neptune is seen in this imaginary view from its moon, Triton.

Between Earth and the sun lie two planets: Venus, closest to the Earth, and Mercury, closest to the sun. Beyond the *orbit* of Earth lies the small planet Mars, which appears to glow red when viewed through a telescope. Mercury, Venus, Earth, and Mars have solid surfaces. The biggest is Earth, with a diameter of just over 7,900 miles. The smallest is Mercury, with a diameter of slightly more than 3,000 miles. Mars is not much bigger than Mercury. It has a diameter of 4,200 miles. Venus, however, is almost the same size as Earth and has a diameter of just over 7,500 miles.

These four planets are called *terrestrial planets* because they are rocky bodies like Earth. *Terra* is the Latin word for land. Beyond the outermost terrestrial planet, Mars, is a great expanse of space before the next planet. Jupiter is the first of four giant outer planets and has a diameter of more than 89,000 miles.

All four outer giants are huge balls of gas enclosing small rocky bodies like the terrestrial planets. Jupiter is enormous and could contain 1,000 planets the size of Earth. The others, Saturn, Uranus, and Neptune, are smaller. Yet even the smallest, Neptune, is more than 30,000 miles in diameter.

Between Mars and Jupiter is a vast belt of rocky fragments and debris left over from the formation of the *solar system* about 4,500 million years ago. All the planets and the sun they orbit around were formed at the same time.

This belt of debris, called the *asteroid belt*, has remained between the orbits of Mars and Jupiter all that time.

Beyond the four giant outer planets can be found a maverick planet called Pluto. It is in a highly *elliptical orbit*, which means that the path it follows in orbit around the sun is in the shape of an ellipse. The rest of the planets are in nearly circular paths. Pluto is smaller than our moon and takes 248 years to go once around the sun.

On each orbit, Pluto swoops inside the orbit of Neptune and is no longer the most distant planet in the solar system. It is in that position now and will remain so until it begins to move farther out early in the next century. It will continue to move farther away until it is almost twice as far from the sun as Neptune. Then once again it will start to move back in on its never-ending orbit.

This is the solar system: an arrangement of nine planets, many moons, and asteroids around a sun that gives out energy for all life on Earth. It is not surprising that since people began to gaze at the heavens, they have found them fascinating and wondrous to observe. It is also not a surprise that when space travel became reality, people wanted to explore.

This artist's impression imagines what it would be like to see the ringed planet Saturn and four of its moons from a fifth moon, Rhea.

Far out on the frozen edge of the solar system, an imaginary view looking back from the surface of Pluto at a dim sun more than four million miles away.

Sister Planets

Chesley Bonestell

Artists imagined that the surface of the planet Mercury would be roasted by the rays of the sun, with rocks parched and cracked by the great heat.

Venus is the closest planet to Earth. It comes to within 26 million miles of us and, aside from the moon, is the closest object in the solar system. Earth and Venus are just over two light minutes apart at their closest point.

Venus has been observed since the beginning of time. Because it is inside the orbit of the Earth, it is situated closer to the sun than the outer planets. We look in toward the sun to see it from our position outside the orbit of Venus. We cannot look directly at Venus when it crosses the disc of the sun. The brilliant light completely destroys all sight of Venus. When it is to one side of the sun, however, we see it as an early evening

When the unmanned robot Viking landed on Mars it found a rocky, dusty surface similar to the moon. Mercury may be similar.

Some regions of the surface of Mercury may look like the surface of Mars, seen here in an artist's impression.

Beneath the dense layers of gas and clouds that completely cover the surface, Venus is known to be much hotter than Mercury because its dense atmosphere traps heat that would otherwise escape into space.

or an early morning object in the sky before it disappears over the horizon.

Venus has been a puzzle for centuries because it is difficult to observe and also because it appears to have no surface markings at all. If it did have markings that were visible from Earth, astronomers could accurately measure how long it takes for Venus to spin once on its axis. By measuring the time taken for the markings to make one complete turn, we could tell how fast it rotated. This would be its "day" compared to Earth's day, which is, of course, about 24 hours.

The reason astronomers cannot see any markings is that the planet is constantly shrouded in dense clouds, and these clouds

13

completely hide the planet's features. Looking at Venus is like looking at a smooth table tennis ball. Because Venus is almost the same size as Earth and its orbit around the sun is closer than that of any other planet, Venus has been called a sister planet to Earth. In fact, nothing could be further from the truth.

For one thing, Venus is the only planet in the solar system that spins backwards. Its "day," the time taken for it to make one complete revolution, is longer that its "year," the time taken for it to travel once around the sun. Venus goes around the sun in just under 225 Earth days, but it takes 243 days to spin once on its polar axis. It is the only planet in the solar system with a longer day than year. If the planet were not continually shrouded in cloud, the sun on Venus

Violent activity in the atmosphere of Venus may be similar to that at the surface of Mars; here a major storm is blowing up dust clouds.

would appear to rise in the west and set in the east. On Earth it rises in the east and sets in the west.

This is not the only aspect of Venus to make it different from Earth. Venus has a dense atmosphere of almost total carbon dioxide. To humans this gas is poisonous, no human could breath it and live. Also, the pressure of the atmosphere at the surface of Venus is a staggering 100 times the pressure of Earth's atmosphere. This means the atmosphere squeezes everything around with a pressure of

1,500 pounds per square inch. No human being could survive without being crushed.

The temperature at Venus's surface is almost 900 degrees. This is hot enough to melt lead. If a human being could stand on the surface of Venus, the view would be a nightmare scene. Everything around would be hotter than a baking oven, the ground parched without a trace of moisture. The sky would have a dull brown glow with a pale yellow haze hanging like a fog. Every so often a fine mist of acid rain would fall, and *sulphur* would ooze through cracks in the rocks. It would not be a pleasant place to be.

Unlike Venus, Mars has a thin atmosphere less than one hundredth the density of Earth's atmosphere.

Mariners to Venus

Two factors about Venus made it a prime target for early spacecraft. For one thing, it was quite close to Earth, and the spacecraft would not have to survive the vacuum of space for long to succeed at sending back information. For another, it was one of the more mysterious planets, because nobody could see down to the surface. When the National Aeronautics and Space Administration (*NASA*), was formed in 1958 to look after the nation's non-military space projects, Venus was at the top of the exploration list.

From the beginning, the *Jet Propulsion Laboratory* in Pasadena, California, was the home of planetary exploration. Known simply as

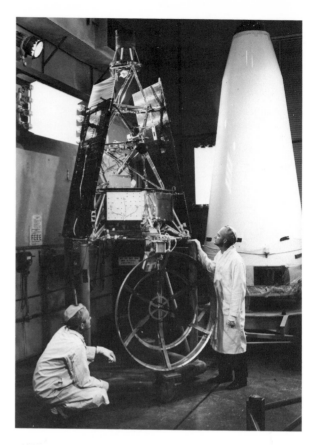

In 1962, NASA engineers prepared the tiny Mariner spacecraft for its long voyage to Venus.

Mariner 1 **failed shortly after launch, and** *Mariner 2* **was the first successful space probe to fly past Venus.**

JPL, the laboratory was a part of the California Institute of Technology. NASA took over several projects that JPL was working on for the army, including planetary probes. The resulting projects grew and expanded. They were kept at JPL and managed there. Over the years the laboratory provided some of the most outstanding discoveries in the solar system through Mariner and Voyager spacecraft built and designed there.

JPL developed a spacecraft design that served as the basis for early missions to the moon and the first mission to Venus. It was economical to use the same technology for both missions. A few parts would have to be changed, but the basic idea worked for both missions. There was no time to waste. The relative motion

16

of the Earth and Venus around the sun provided an opportunity to launch spacecraft to that planet only once every nineteen months. The opportunity would last only a few weeks and would not come again for nearly two years.

There was little time to get the spacecraft ready, but it was completed by early 1962 for launch during July 1962. It was called *Mariner 1*, and it was launched on an Atlas-Agena rocket. Shortly after lift-off, the rocket ran amok and had to be intentionally blown up to prevent it from straying into populated areas and crashing. The back-up spacecraft was readied, and *Mariner 2* was successfully launched on August 27, 1962.

There had been earlier missions to Venus, but none had been successful. A Soviet probe called *Venera 1* had been launched in February 1961, but its communication link failed, and nothing more was heard of it. *Mariner 2* sped on its way, and tracking stations on Earth kept in contact. It was exploring areas of space no other probe had visited, and instruments on board recorded

Electrical test equipment and computers help scientists and engineers check out the various systems aboard the spacecraft.

The *Mariner 1* and *2* spacecraft were the first designed by NASA to leave Earth and journey to another planet; great care was taken in the assembly of these delicate objects.

18

details about radiation coming from the sun.

Mariner 2 was small. It weighed only 447 pounds and consisted of a tower frame resting on a box of electronic systems. Two *solar panels* carried 9,800 cells for converting sunlight into electrical energy, and these provided 200 watts. That is about one-quarter the energy given off by a small electric room heater. The panels were each 5 feet in length and 2 feet, 5 inches wide. From the lower section of the equipment base to the top of the tower, the spacecraft stood 12 feet tall.

A small rocket motor was attached to the base so that a correction to the course, called the *trajectory,* could be made. After the Atlas-Agena had safely placed *Mariner 2* on its trajectory to Venus, tracking stations reported that it would miss the planet by 231,000 miles. It was not supposed to hit Venus but pass above it, enabling scanning instruments on board to observe the planet and send this information back.

On September 4, 1962, the course correction motor was fired for just under 28 seconds. That changed the spacecraft's direction very slightly and allowed it to head for a near miss of 21,500 miles. *Mariner 2* reached that point on December 14, 1962, when it flew past Venus and

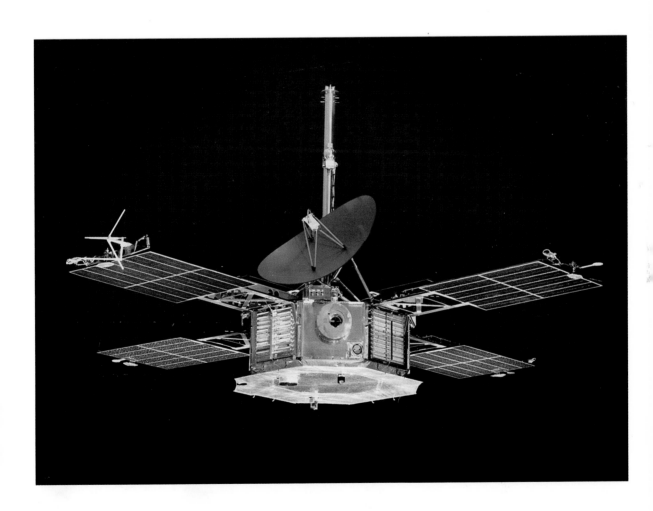

Launched in June 1967, *Mariner 5* **flew by Venus at an altitude of 2,500 miles just over four months later.**

recorded a surface temperature of almost 900 degrees. It did so by measuring the reflected *microwave energy* from the surface. Microwaves are radio waves that travel right through the clouds. From Mariner measurements, the clouds on Venus were calculated to start at a height of 45 miles from the surface and to end at 60 miles.

Mariner 2 had been a great success. It was the world's first planetary encounter with a robot spacecraft launched from Earth and a true milestone in the history of spaceflight. The Soviets had been trying desperately to get a probe to Venus. They launched four in all during 1961 and 1962, and all failed for various technical reasons. The U.S. now turned its attention to Mars and successfully flew *Mariner 4* to that planet in 1964. *Mariner 3* had failed to get into space because of a problem with the shroud covering the spacecraft at launch. The back-up spacecraft for that mission was re-designed into the next probe to Venus and called *Mariner 5*.

Meanwhile, the Soviets achieved success with their *Venera 3* spacecraft when it struck the

The *Mariner 5* spacecraft was based on the successful *Mariner 4* design seen here, the first space probe to fly past Mars.

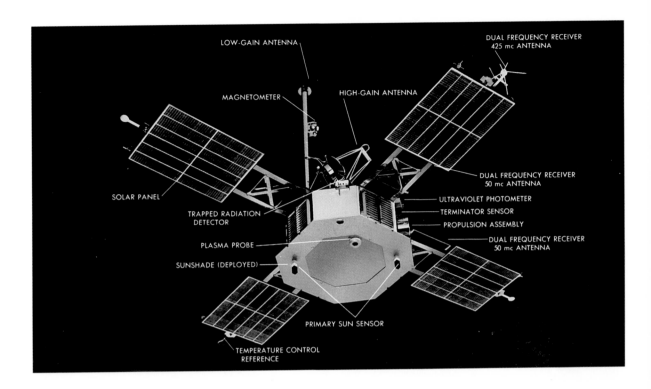

LOW-GAIN ANTENNA

DUAL FREQUENCY RECEIVER
425 mc ANTENNA

MAGNETOMETER

HIGH-GAIN ANTENNA

DUAL FREQUENCY RECEIVER
50 mc ANTENNA

ULTRAVIOLET PHOTOMETER

TERMINATOR SENSOR

PROPULSION ASSEMBLY

DUAL FREQUENCY RECEIVER
50 mc ANTENNA

SOLAR PANEL

TRAPPED RADIATION
DETECTOR

PLASMA PROBE

SUNSHADE (DEPLOYED)

PRIMARY SUN SENSOR

TEMPERATURE CONTROL
REFERENCE

The *Mariner 5* spacecraft had smaller solar panels than the Mars Mariner because it was flying closer to the sun and would not need as many solar cells for its electrical power.

The small green dish on top of the *Mariner 5* spacecraft was used to transmit information from the probe's scientific instruments directly back to Earth.

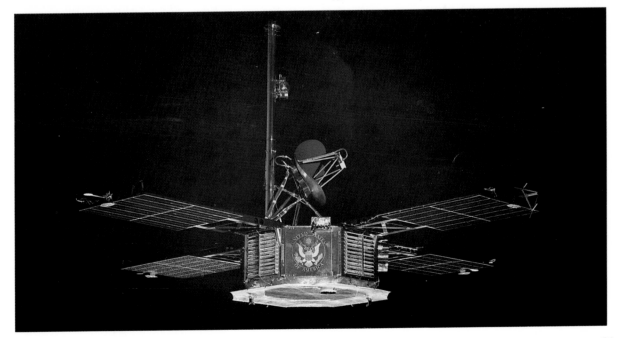

In 1973, following its spacecraft missions to the planet Mars, NASA returned to Venus with *Mariner 10,* a spacecraft that would also journey on to Mercury.

surface of Venus on March 1, 1966, becoming the first man-made object to reach another planet. It did not survive the crash. Launched in June 1967, *Venera 4* dropped an egg-shaped capsule weighing 846 pounds into the atmosphere of Venus. It was intended to survive, but as it descended increasing temperature and pressures caused it to fail at a height of 15 miles from the surface. It was, nevertheless, the first direct measurement of the dense carbon-dioxide atmosphere.

Mariner 5 was launched to Venus on June 14, 1967. The spacecraft was alone and had no back-up, because it had been the back-up to the Mariner-Mars mission. The spacecraft weighed 550 pounds and stood just over 9 feet tall to the top of its communication antenna. Four solar panels were arranged in the form of an X and spanned 18 feet. As they had been on *Mariner 2,* the solar panels were folded during launch and only opened after the spacecraft separated from the rocket that launched it.

Mariner 5 missed Venus by 2,440 miles in October 1967, just a day after *Venera 4* dropped its capsule to the atmosphere. It confirmed everything that earlier spacecraft had measured. A technical report from NASA's Jet Propulsion Laboratory summed it up: "Venus appears to offer roasting heat, a choking atmosphere, crushing pressure, and murky skies, to which forbidding weather and hostile terrain may perhaps be added."

This mosaic of several pictures of the Earth pasted together was taken during November 1973 by *Mariner 10's* two television cameras operating at 42-second intervals.

Double Shot

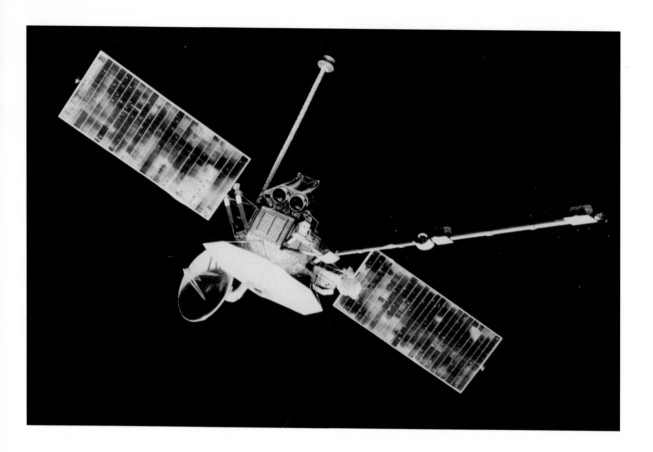

Mariner 10 was more complex than previous designs and was specially built to survive the intense temperatures close to the sun, where it would travel to reach the planet Mercury.

For a while, NASA turned its attention away from the planet Venus. NASA was anxious to achieve success with Mars, because that planet seemed to be a possible candidate for life. The space agency wanted to send a robot spacecraft to land on the surface during the late 1970s to find out if there was life on that planet. Accordingly, mapping missions to Mars were flown in 1969 and 1971. Then it was Venus's turn once again. This time, a single Mariner spacecraft went to two planets, Venus and Mercury.

The double shot was made possible by using the *gravity* of Venus to bend the trajectory of the spacecraft and throw it like a slingshot off to Mercury, the innermost planet of them all. This

was the only mission to Mercury by either the United States or the Soviet Union, and it was a valuable chance to look closely at one of the more mysterious planets in the solar system.

Because it is inside the orbit of Earth, Venus can be seen only during early evening or early morning. Mercury is even less visible, because it is inside the orbit of Venus and even closer to the sun. Mercury is the smallest of the terrestrial planets and orbits the sun from a distance of

Cameras were carried primarily to get good shots of the planet Mercury but passing Venus in February 1974, *Mariner 10* took this view of the densely cloud-shrouded planet.

From measurements taken remotely by U.S. and Soviet spacecraft, Venus is known to have a very dense atmosphere of carbon dioxide where temperatures at the surface reach more than 800 degrees.

The surface of Venus is believed to have been shaped by violent events early in its history and to have evolved very differently to Mars or the Earth.

about 36 million miles. Venus orbits the sun at a distance of 67 million miles and Earth at about 93 million miles. Because Mercury is so close to the sun, it is extremely hot. It is not, however, as hot as Venus. The dense atmosphere of Venus acts like a greenhouse and traps heat, raising the temperature far higher than if the planet were without atmosphere.

Mercury has no atmosphere to distribute the heat from one side of the planet to the other. It is

Although Venus' surface is not directly visible, radar from Earth and space has mapped the surface, revealing great mountain ranges, canyons, and huge craters.

like the moon, only bigger. Its temperature on the sunlit side is about 650 degrees and dips to −300 degrees on the night side of the planet. Like Earth, Venus has even temperatures with very little difference between the day and night sides. Mercury is a heavy planet for its size and has about the same density as the Earth. A cubic foot of Mercury would, on average, weigh about the same as a cubic foot of Earth. Compared to Earth, Venus is a little lighter.

Mercury has a lot of iron and heavy metal in its interior. The moon is much lighter per cubic foot than Earth is and is made of lighter materials, including *aluminum and titanium*. Mercury is, in fact, more like Earth inside, with a surface more like the moon. Because of these

differences and similarities, scientists were eager to get a good view of the planet with cameras. There was little point in taking cameras to Venus, since the surface is completely obscured by clouds.

One feature of the orbit of Mercury and the period of its day fascinates scientists. Mercury takes 88 Earth days to travel once around the sun. In other words, the length of a "year" on Mercury is 88 Earth days. It takes Mercury 58.6 Earth days to spin once on its polar axis, completing one "day". For every three complete revolutions on its axis, the planet makes two orbits of the sun. Because the speed of rotation is so slow, Mercury would present the same side to the sun for 180 Earth days. On Mercury, the sun would gradually shift from east to west, remaining in the sky for more than 3 Earth months.

Because the sun seems to move so slowly across the sky, the surface would bake in the heat for months before night came and temperatures fell. The planners of *Mariner 10's* voyage knew that heat would present a major problem for the spacecraft. *Mariner 10* would fly closer to the sun than any previous spacecraft, and its proximity to the sun would call for extraordinary protective measures. NASA devised a special blanket on the side facing the sun to protect delicate instruments and a shield to keep the temperatures under control.

The spacecraft had two solar cell panels and would be tilted increasingly away from the sun as it flew closer to the planet Mercury. This would keep temperatures on the panels down to around 210 degrees and prevent the sun from scorching them. Overall, *Mariner 10* was basically an eight-sided box with two enormous telescopic cameras on top and two solar panels

By studying the surface features on Mercury, scientists are able to better understand the early history of the solar system.

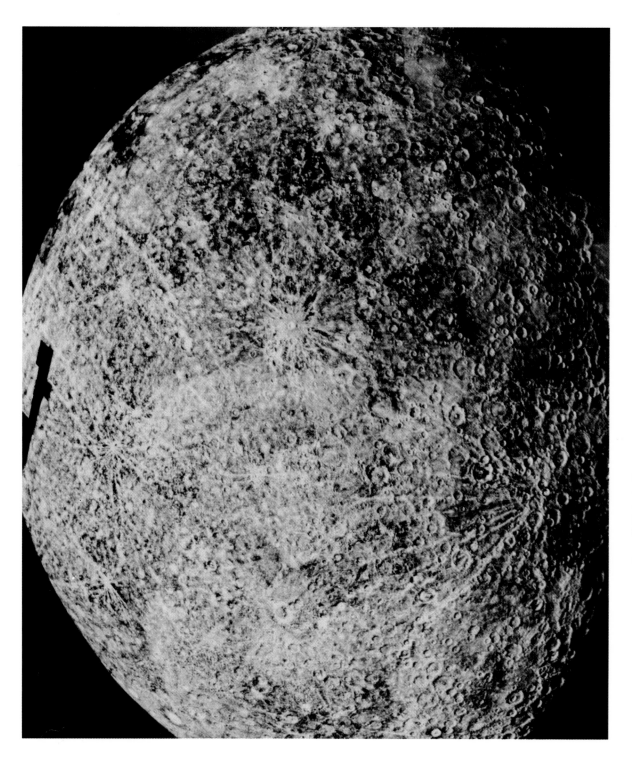

When *Mariner 10* flew past Mercury in 1974, its cameras took this mosaic of pictures revealing many craters caused by rocks and boulders smashing into the surface early in its history.

Seen here in a picture taken by *Apollo 8,* the moon is covered with large, dark, dried lava lakes, unlike anything seen on Mercury.

on opposite sides. The cameras were equipped with special filters to control the amount of light coming in and could take wide or narrow angle shots. The spacecraft had a small rocket motor for course changes during and after the flight to Mercury. At launch the spacecraft had a weight of 1,109 pounds, including propellant for the rocket motor to make course corrections.

Mariner 10 set off on its historic journey on November 3, 1973. Its first target was a close pass by Venus at precisely the right distance to get flung off to Mercury. Gravity at Venus would bend the flight path by the right amount for the spacecraft to change course without burning any rocket fuel. It was like a game of interplanetary billiards, bouncing the spacecraft off the gravity field of one planet to fly by another.

Mariner 10 performed well all the way to Venus

and flew by the planet at a distance of 3,595 miles on February 5, 1974. It was able to use its powerful cameras to shoot a series of stunning pictures. These showed the cloud tops of the planet in several different colors using filters on the camera lenses. Never before had a

The moon's dried lava lakes provide a relatively smooth surface on which to land, like this site where the first manned moon landing took place.

spacecraft to Venus been equipped for such magnificent photography. It showed nothing of the surface but plenty of action in the atmosphere.

Because weight is always at a premium in spacecraft, unnecessary instruments have to be left off. While scientists would have liked even more pictures of the clouds, the weight allocated for scientific instruments was given over to instruments that could provide more information. Only because *Mariner 10* was primarily built to observe Mercury with TV

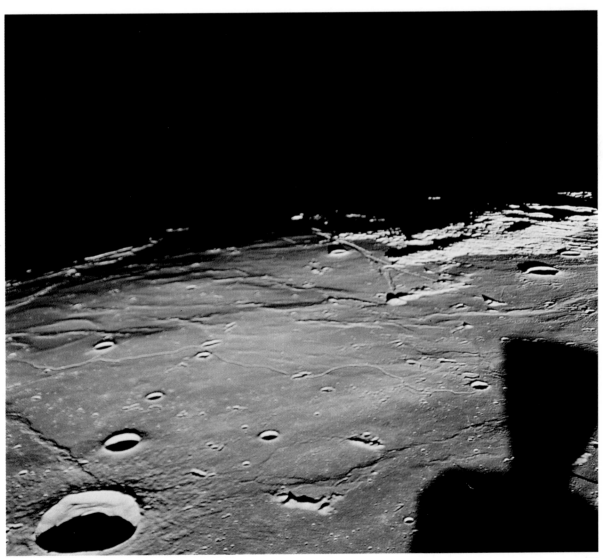

No great lava lakes are seen on Mercury; instead the entire surface is densely littered with impact craters.

cameras could scientists get their pictures of Venus on the way.

Mariner 10 discovered that there were vast *circulation bands* in the atmosphere of Venus. These bands appeared to rotate with the planet. There was evidence, too, of large amounts of heat rising up through the atmosphere from the lower levels to the cloud tops. This was not surprising, given the tremendous temperatures at the bottom of the atmosphere close to the surface.

Mariner 10 sped on to Mercury, going where no other spacecraft had ever been before. Venus would be left to Russian probes for the next four years. On March 16, 1974, a course correction

The dark areas on the moon were caused by large flows of lava oozing through cracks in the surface and covering vast areas to a depth of several miles.

was made using the on-board rocket motor. Accuracy was vital. An error of 3,200 feet in the miss distance at Venus would result in an error of 620 miles at Mercury. As it was, after passing Venus, *Mariner 10* was aiming for a point 6,200 miles away from the planet. The course correction narrowed that distance to just 437 miles.

With more than 3 million miles still to go, *Mariner 10's* powerful cameras were turned on and began taking pictures of Mercury on March

23. As it approached and passed the planet, the spacecraft shot more than 2,000 pictures of the sunlit side, taking half that side on the way in and the other half on the way out. What Mariner sent back were fantastic pictures of a moon-like surface, cracked and blistered under the terrific heat of the sun. There were many differences between the moon and Mercury, and scientists anxiously awaited the next part of the mission.

Engineers had always hoped that if *Mariner 10* survived and passed Mercury, it would make a return trip to take more pictures. They now put that plan into practice. Because *Mariner 10* passed so close to Mercury, the course of the spacecraft was changed into an elliptical orbit of the sun. It was a mini-planet all its own, traveling around the sun between the orbit of Mercury at

Taken during the second encounter with Mercury in September 1974, from a range of 47,000 miles, this picture shows ridges and cliffs more than a mile high.

Although the moon, seen here, appears similar to Mercury, the movement of hot lava across the surface is more readily visible than on Mercury.

the low point and almost out to the orbit of Venus at the most distant point.

A couple of course corrections tweaked up the orbit precisely for a fly-by of Mercury at a distance of 29,700 miles on September 21, 1974. Almost 2,000 pictures were shot that time. Unfortunately, a penalty for trimming the path of the spacecraft into a return orbit was that the spacecraft returned to pass the planet when the exact same side was sunlit as on the first pass.

A third pass was made on March 16, 1975,

when about 1,100 pictures were taken of this barren, baked world. This time, *Mariner 10* came within 193 miles of the surface for a really close shave that called for accurate course maneuvers. *Mariner 10* shot the best and closest pictures of its mission and sent back to Earth almost 1,100 images. It had been a breath-taking tour of the solar system's innermost world. The spacecraft is still there, going endlessly around the sun, but it will never go back to Mercury again.

Pioneer

NASA returned to the planet Venus in 1978 with a mission designed to provide detailed information about the atmosphere. Instead of flying past the planet and scanning it with instruments, a spacecraft called Pioneer-Venus would drop probes through the clouds and directly measure temperature, pressure, and the composition of the gases. A second Pioneer spacecraft would put itself into orbit around Venus and map the surface with *radar*.

Radar works by sending out a radio signal

receiving it back after it has been reflected from a solid surface. Careful measurement of the time taken for it to return builds up a picture of the height of different features on the surface. This process eventually produces a picture of the surface not unlike a photograph. Each dot that makes up the radar picture requires a separate sounding of the surface, so the process is time-consuming. It is, however, the only way to "see" a surface totally covered with cloud.

The probe-carrying spacecraft and the orbiter spacecraft were each built around a drum-shaped cylinder 8 feet in diameter and 3 feet, 11 inches tall. Four probes were carried on the top of one drum. One large probe, 5 feet in diameter and weighing almost 700 pounds, was in the middle. It was surrounded by three smaller probes, each 2 feet, 7 inches in diameter and weighing 198 pounds. The probes would be released into different parts of the planet, and the main drum-shaped

The Pioneer-Venus orbiter (right) was launched in May 1978, and arrived at the planet in December, while the probes (left) were launched in August and arrived five days after the orbiter.

To get a better understanding of Venus, NASA returned to that planet in 1978 with two spacecraft: one was designed to go into orbit and the other to drop four probes through the atmosphere to the surface.

An artist's imaginary view as the spacecraft that carried the probes to Venus burns up in the outer regions of the planet's atmosphere.

spacecraft would continue to send scientific information as it plunged into the cloud tops. The Pioneer with the probes weighed almost one ton at launch. The orbiter would weigh almost 1,300 pounds.

The orbiter carried a large rocket motor to reduce its speed as it swept past Venus, allowing gravity to overcome the speed of the spacecraft and pull it into orbit. From there it would send back information from many instruments and make radar maps of the surface far below. It weighed 1,283 pounds at

launch and with its antenna mast up, stood almost 15 feet high. Both probe and orbiter spacecraft obtained electrical power from solar cells wrapped around the sides of each drum.

First off the launch pad was the orbiter, which left on May 20, 1978. It made it safely to Venus and dropped into orbit on December 4. This orbit was highly elliptical, coming as close as 233 miles above the surface of the planet before sweeping out in a long arc to a height of more than 41,500 miles. From there it swept down to the low pass again before starting

This is an artist's imaginary view of Venus' largest highland region, named Aphrodite, a continent-sized feature as large as half of Africa.

The highest and most dramatic continent-sized region on Venus, called Ishtar Terra, stands up to ten miles above the surrounding area; it is compared in this illustration with the continental United States.

Two huge volcanoes tower six miles above the great plains of Venus.

another orbit. As the experiments got under way, the Pioneer spacecraft carrying the probes approached Venus.

The probe Pioneer had been launched on August 8, 1978, but on a faster course to Venus. It arrived only five days after the orbiter dropped into its continuous path around the planet. The four probes were released as the spacecraft was homing in on the planet from a distance of 8 million miles. The larger one descended on the sunlit side at the equator. One of the smaller probes entered the atmosphere on the sunlit side toward the north pole, while the other two entered on the dark side.

The larger probe had parachutes to slow its descent. The parachutes were jettisoned at a height of 29 miles and the probe fell freely to the surface of the planet. Its speed was broken by the dense carbon-dioxide gas. One of the small probes on the sunlit side of the planet survived all the way to the surface and continued to send back information for 67 minutes. These probes were designed for the unusual conditions at Venus. Meanwhile, the orbiter continued its endless journey around Venus and began to compile a detailed radar map.

The orbiter discovered mountains that rise 26,000 feet above the plains; one mountain, which scientists named Maxwell, rises more than 36,000 feet. This is much higher than

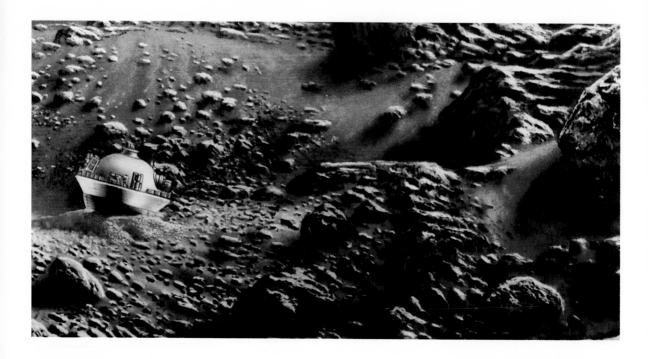

Earth's Mt. Everest, which is 29,000 feet above sea level and less when measured from the plateau on which it stands. Giant craters up to 375 miles across were discovered, and great depressions in the surface were apparently filled with lakes of *lava*. The lava probably oozed through surface cracks and became solid on the surface when it "cooled" to the planet's temperature of well over 800 degrees.

By this time, the Soviets had already landed several capsules on Venus. After several failed attempts, *Venera 7* reported back from the surface for a few minutes after it landed on December 15, 1970. Then *Venera 9* and *Venera 10* landed in June 1975 and took pictures for several minutes. As expected, the surface was bleak with cracked boulders and slabs of jagged rock. *Venera 11* and *Venera 12* were sent up in 1978, and each put landers down to the surface. If any pictures were taken at that time, none were released by the Soviets.

In 1981, the Soviets launched *Venera 13* and *Venera 14*, and both sent back a few color pictures. They returned to Earth by radio signal information about the atmosphere of the planet. The tops of the clouds were covered

Like the Pioneer-Venus probes, Soviet spacecraft have reached the surface of Venus and sent back information about the atmosphere and its temperature.

with a layer of smog more than 9 miles thick. The bulk of the clouds appeared to lie between 30 and 35 miles above Venus, although some images from the Pioneer orbiter showed clouds up to 40 miles high. These clouds were mainly sulphuric acid and sulphur dioxide, which are harmful and unpleasant chemicals.

Winds around Venus are very high. The gases in the upper atmosphere move around the planet in just four days. Given the slow rotation of the planet on its axis, this means they are moving at a speed of more than 200 MPH all the time. At a height of 30 miles, wind speed is down to around 120 MPH, and at 12 miles only 50 MPH. There is almost no wind at all at the surface. The orbiter carried a special imaging instrument similar to a camera, and more than 1,000 views were taken of the clouds.

This artist's impression shows the lowest regions of Venus. The bottom of this giant rift valley sinks about four miles below the surrounding area.

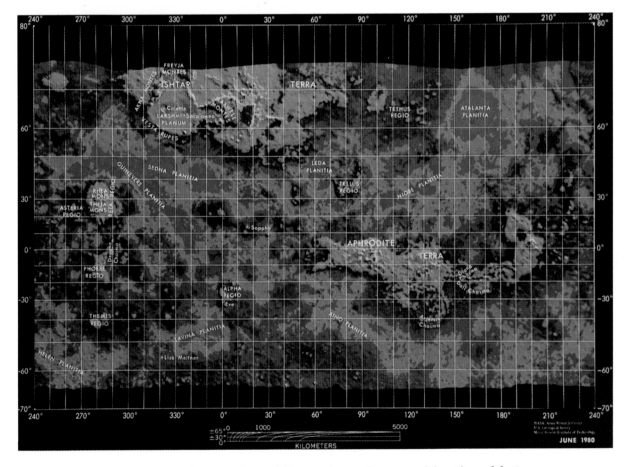

This radar map of the surface of Venus shows the general location of features identified to date.

41

Future Missions

The Pioneer orbiter completed its radar mapping and continued to take measurements of the atmosphere remotely with scanning instruments on the spacecraft. Changes to the orbit were made from time to time, using the on-board rocket thrusters. In 1988, the spacecraft completed ten years of duty and was still going strong. Scientists believe the spacecraft may continue to operate until 1992, when its fuel runs out and it can no longer make important course corrections to the orbit.

The Soviets launched *Venera 15* and *Venera 16* in 1983, and they were placed in orbit around the planet several months later. This was the first time the Soviets had put spacecraft into orbit around Venus. Each craft carried a radar unit to perform mapping duties similar to the Pioneer orbiter launched five years earlier. The Soviets gathered detailed information about surface features and exchanged data with the United States. Scientists from both countries compared information to build up a better picture of what the planet and its atmosphere is really like.

In December 1984, the Soviets launched two Vega spacecraft. Each consisted of a fly-by spacecraft carrying a balloon packed in a special canister and a Venus lander. As each spacecraft approached Venus, it released its balloon canister and the lander. The landers descended to the surface, and the balloons were inflated to float around in the atmosphere. The spacecraft flew past Venus to meet up with Halley's Comet, which returned to the Earth's region of the solar system in 1986 for the first time in 76 years.

In 1989, NASA intends to launch a Magellan spacecraft to Venus. It will be equipped with a powerful radar scanner to carry out extensive radar mapping from orbit around the planet. If

From its position in orbit around Venus, *Magellan* **gets a "view" of surface features because radio waves, unlike visible light, can penetrate down to the surface.**

Pioneer is still operating, this will be the first time NASA has had two spacecraft sending back data from Venus simultaneously. Magellan is about 21 feet high and carries two solar cell panels for electrical power. The spacecraft weighs almost 4 tons at launch and will be taken to Earth orbit first by the shuttle. From there a rocket motor will boost it toward Venus.

The Soviets want to go back to Venus in 1991, Their spacecraft, called Vesta, would be launched in two sections joined together. One section would detach itself as the combination approached Venus and descend through the

NASA's *Magellan* spacecraft launched by shuttle in 1989 was designed to map the surface features of Venus by radio signals bounced off the surface.

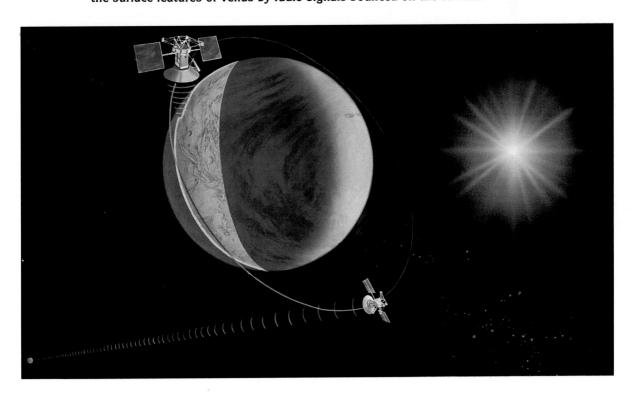

Information taken on each orbit of the planet is sent back by *Magellan* to scientists on Earth.

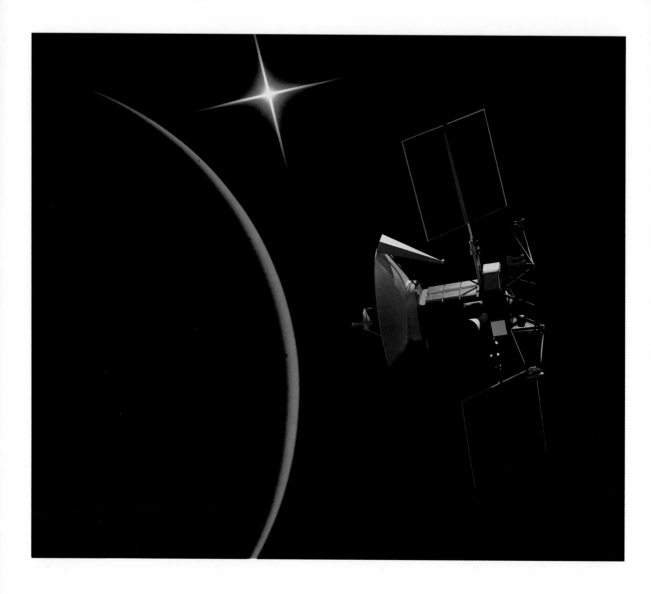

Like earlier Mariner and Pioneer spacecraft to Venus, *Magellan* gets its power from sunlight converted into electrical energy through solar cells on wing-like panels.

atmosphere to land on the surface. During the descent it would take pictures of the ground as it gradually approached a landing. Special instruments would measure the atmosphere on the way down and on the surface. The lander would be much bigger and more advanced than the landers used previously.

The other part of the spacecraft would fly past Venus and on to meet up with an asteroid. It would investigate the asteroid with a probe that would land on its surface. In this way, scientists are able to visit two objects, rather than just one. For the foreseeable future, robots will be the only way of exploring Venus. Humans may never go down to that hot, barren surface, but with spacecraft like Pioneer, Magellan, and Vesta, they probably won't need to.

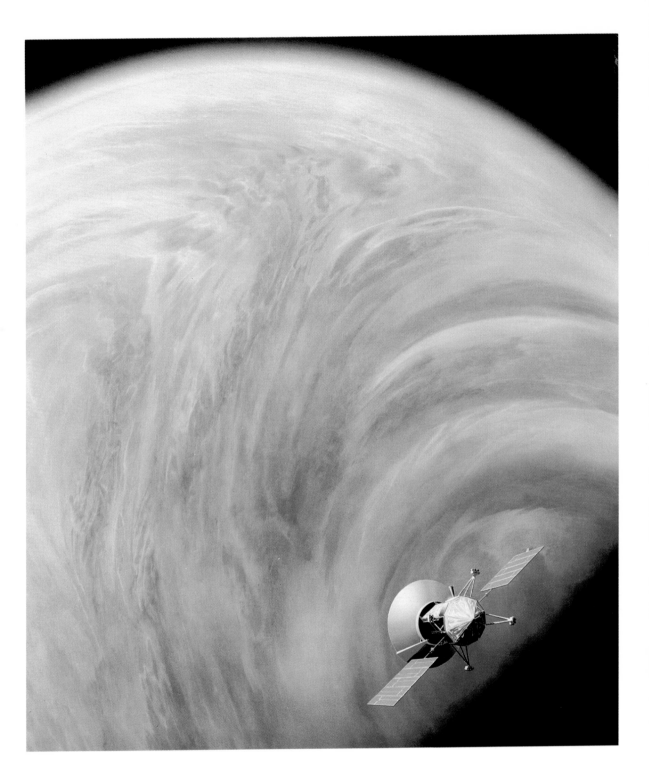

By studying Venus, we are coming to understand the reason for its inhospitable conditions, and that may help us better understand Earth's atmosphere.

GLOSSARY

Aluminum	A light, silvery-white metal element that resists corrosion; aluminum is the third most abundant element in the Earth's crust.
Asteroid belt	A field of rocky debris orbiting the sun between the planets Mars and Jupiter.
Circulation bands	Bands of hot air that encircle Venus and appear to rotate with the planet.
Elliptical orbit	An orbit in which the path of a satellite or spacecraft takes the shape of a flattened circle.
Gravity	The force of attraction that moves or tends to move bodies toward the center of a celestial body such as the Earth or moon.
Jet Propulsion Laboratory (JPL)	Owned and operated by the California Institute of Technology, JPL operates as the mission control center for most planetary missions and is responsible for project management.
Lava	Hot rock and iron materials melted by intense heat inside the Earth.
Microwave energy	Electromagnetic radiation used in radar and cooking.
NASA	National Aeronautics and Space Administration, set up in October 1958 for the peaceful exploration of space.
Orbit	The curved path, usually almost circular, followed by a planet or satellite in its motion around another planet in space.
Radar	**Ra**dio **d**etection **an**d **r**anging. Radio signal are sent out and reflected from a solid object, therebt detecting its presence.
Solar panels	Surfaces to which are attached sensitive cells for converting sunlight into electricity for satellite or spacecraft power.
Solar system	The sun and the bodies held in its gravitational field, including the planets, the asteroids, and comets.
Sulpher	A non-metallic element that occurs naturally in volcanoes.
Terrestrial planets	Planets with solid, rocky surfaces. The name comes from the Latin word *terra,* which means Earth.
Titanium	A strong white metal that is very typically used in the manufacture of strong light alloys.
Trajectory	The path described by an object moving in air or space; the curved path of a missile or spacecraft.

INDEX

Page numbers in *italics* refer to photographs or illustrations.